THE
CHICKASAW

by Craig A. Doherty and Katherine M. Doherty

Illustrated by Richard Smolinski

ROURKE PUBLICATIONS, INC.

VERO BEACH, FLORIDA 32964

CONTENTS

Library of Congress Cataloging-in-Publication Data

Doherty, Katherine M.
    The Chickasaw / by Katherine M. Doherty, Craig A. Doherty.
        p.   cm. — (Native American people)
    Includes bibliographical references and index.
    1. Chickasaw Indians—History—Juvenile literature.
2. Chickasaw Indians—Social life and customs—Juvenile literature. [1. Chickasaw Indians. 2. Indians of North America.] I. Doherty, Craig A. II. Title. III. Series.
E99.C55D64 1994   973'.04973—dc20   93-42163
    ISBN 0-86625-531-1   CIP
                                                 AC

Introduction

For many years, archaeologists—and other people who study early Native American cultures—agreed that the first humans to live in the Americas arrived about 11,500 years ago. These first Americans were believed to have been big-game hunters who lived by hunting the woolly mammoths and giant bison that inhabited the Ice Age plains of the Americas. This widely accepted theory also asserted that these first Americans crossed a land bridge linking Siberia, in Asia, to Alaska. This land bridge occurred when the accumulation of water in Ice Age glaciers lowered the level of the world's oceans.

In recent years, many scientists have challenged this theory. Although most agree that many big-game hunting bands left similar artifacts all over the Americas 11,500 years ago, many now suggest that the first Americans may have arrived as far back as 20,000 or even 50,000 years. There are those who think that some of these earliest Americans may have even come to the Americas by boat, working their way down the west coast of North America and South America.

In support of this theory, scientists who study language or genetics (the study of the inherited similarities and differences found in living things) believe that there may have been more than one period of migration. They also believe that these multiple migrations started in different parts of Asia, which accounts for the genetic and language differences that exist among

the many people of the Americas. Although it is still not certain when the first Americans arrived, most scientists agree that today's Native Americans are the descendants of early Asian immigrants.

Over the thousands of years between the first arrivals from Asia and the introduction of Europeans, the people who were living in the Americas flourished and inhabited every corner of the two continents. Native Americans lived above the Arctic Circle in the North, to Tierra del Fuego at the tip of South America, and from the Atlantic Ocean in the East to the Pacific Ocean in the West.

During this time, the people of North America divided into hundreds of different groups. Each group adapted to the environment in which it lived. As agriculture developed and spread throughout the Americas, some people switched from being nomads to living in one area. In the Southwest, along the Mississippi River, in Mexico, and in Peru, groups of Native Americans built large cities. In other areas, groups continued to exist as hunters and gatherers with no permanent settlements.

In the southeastern part of the United States there lived a number of tribes. These tribes had adapted to the climate of the region and had become excellent farmers who lived in permanent villages. Later, five of these tribes became known as the Five Civilized Tribes. The Chickasaw are one of them. The other four are the Creek, Cherokee, Choctaw, and Seminole. The Chickasaw lived in an area that is now northern Mississippi and Alabama and western Tennessee.

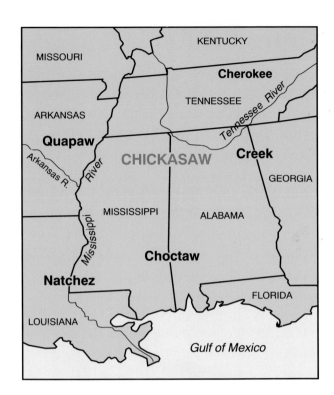

Origins of the Chickasaw

There have been people in the southeastern United States for at least 10,000 years. Many of these people were nomadic. They moved through the region with the seasons, gathering wild plants, hunting, and fishing. About 1,000 years ago, they learned to grow corn. Corn had been developed from a wild plant by the Native Americans in Central America. As the importance of corn increased, people were able to settle in one area.

According to the Chickasaw story of their origin, they once lived farther west. Two of their leaders, Chicsa and Chacta, led the people east until they reached a land that suited them. Then they split into two groups. The people who settled with Chicsa became the Chickasaw. The people who settled with Chacta became the Choctaw.

Scientists cannot verify the Chickasaw legend, but the Choctaw and Chickasaw languages are so similar they are convinced that at one time these tribes were one people. Native American languages are grouped together in language families. A language family contains the languages that descended from one common language. The Chickasaw and Choctaw languages are part of the Muskogean family, which in turn is part of a larger family of Gulf languages. A number of different tribes spoke Muskogean languages. These tribes lived throughout the Southeast.

Daily Life

A traditional Chickasaw home usually consisted of three buildings—a summer house, a winter house, and a granary. The granary was where the Chickasaw stored corn and other food. The Chickasaw built two houses so that they would be comfortable all year.

Summer houses were designed to keep people cool during the hot months. Usually ten to fifteen feet wide and twenty to twenty-five feet long, they were customarily divided into two rooms. They had porches on either end, and a gabled roof covered

A Chickasaw warrior rests in his summer home.

with bark or grass thatch. The walls were made of woven mats and the mats had holes in them to let the air circulate.

The winter houses, built to keep people warm during the colder months, were usually circular and about twenty-five feet in diameter. The floor of the winter house was dug approximately three feet deep. The walls were made by weaving saplings together and then covering both the outside and the inside with a thick layer of clay and grass. The Chickasaw often finished by whitewashing those walls, as well. The roof of the winter house was always thatched.

Inside, Chickasaw houses were very sparsely furnished. Sleeping platforms, which were placed next to the walls,

were made with poles and then covered with mats and furs. There were stools to sit on, but the rest of the furnishings consisted only of the tools and other utensils necessary for everyday life. The Chickasaw lived with one nuclear family per household, much as we do today. A nuclear family consists of a mother, a father, and their children.

Family Life

The Chickasaw tribe was matriarchal. That means the children of the Chickasaw were considered part of their mother's family. All Chickasaw were members of a clan. When children were born, they became members of their mother's clan. Teaching young

boys the ways of the tribe was the responsibility of their mother's brothers. Young girls were taught by their mothers and her sisters.

From the earliest ages, boys and girls were treated very differently. Boys were expected to grow up to be good hunters and fierce warriors. Girls were expected to be good at domestic tasks, such as taking care of children. Young boys spent much of their time learning how to hunt and fight, while young girls helped their mothers in the fields and in preparing food.

Successful Chickasaw people often had slaves. Chickasaw slaves were other Native Americans who had been captured by Chickasaw warriors. There was only one way a Chickasaw woman could escape the hard work of

A winter house (left) and a granary (right) were two of the three year-round buildings the Chickasaw used.

the fields, and that was if her husband was a successful warrior and brought home enough slaves to do all the menial work. The Chickasaw would cut some of the tendons in the feet of their slaves. This way the slaves could work but were unable to run away.

Marriage and courtship among the Chickasaw was direct. When a young Chickasaw man wanted to marry, he would find a young woman of another clan and offer her a small gift. If the woman accepted the gift, she was interested in him. After a short courtship, they would marry in a very simple ceremony.

During a Chickasaw wedding, the bride and groom would stand before witnesses. The groom would bring an ear of corn. He would break it in two and give half to the bride. After this ceremony they were married.

Food

The Chickasaw, who grew much of the food they ate, had communal fields that the whole village shared. Each family also had its own garden. Corn was one of the most important crops, along with peas, beans, squash, melons, sunflowers, and pumpkins. The Chickasaw also grew tobacco.

When the corn was ripe, the Chickasaw roasted ears of it fresh. Corn that was not eaten fresh was dried and stored, to be eaten in a variety of ways during the rest of the year. Dried corn kernels were ground for breads, porridge, and hominy. To grind corn, the Chickasaw used a hollowed-out hickory log and a long wooden pestle. The main staple of the diet, soups and stews, consisted of corn and other vegetables. Whatever meat the hunters brought home was added to these dishes.

The Chickasaw often ate meat called venison, the meat from a deer. They believed that people were like the animals they ate. Although the Chickasaw hunted bears, the meat of the swift and agile deer was preferred over that of the slow and lumbering bear. Venison was eaten fresh. Any extra was dried or smoked and added to stews at a later time. Fish was also included in the Chickasaw diet.

Opposite: A Chickasaw wedding ceremony.
Below: A common tool for grinding corn was the mortar and pestle.

Hunting and Fishing

Next to being a warrior, the most important part of a Chickasaw man's life was hunting. Hunting was considered a sacred activity and the hunters often asked for assistance from the spirits. Deer, the primary targets of Chickasaw hunters, were hunted using the bow and arrow. Chickasaw hunters also killed deer and smaller animals using blow guns.

Deer were not only an important source of food. Antlers were made into arrowheads and other tools. Deer hides were turned into clothes. Deer sinew (tendons) were used to make bow strings and thread for sewing.

Bears were also hunted by the Chickasaw. Although the Chickasaw preferred to eat deer, other products from the bear were very important. Bearskins became warm winter robes and bedding. Bearhide, much thicker than deerhide, was used for moccasins. Bear gut was made into bow strings that were the favorites of Chickasaw hunters.

The Chickasaw women rendered, or melted, the fat of the bear to obtain oil for cooking. The Chickasaw also used bear oil on their hair. Sassafras and cinnamon were added to the oil, which allowed the Chickasaw to store the bear oil for long periods of time, keeping it fresh. Even bear claws were saved, drilled, and used for jewelry.

The area the Chickasaw lived in had streams and rivers filled with fish at certain times of the year. The Chickasaw

Opposite: One of the most important natural resources for the Chickasaw was the deer, providing food, clothing, and tools.

used a number of different techniques to catch the fish. They built cane fish traps, or cast nets in deep spots where they knew fish swam. In one unusual technique, they even drugged the fish. A concoction of devil's shoestring (an herb), walnut hulls, and buckeye was put in the river where fish were suspected to be. The fish drug, which stunned but did not kill the fish, caused them to rise to the surface, where they were easily speared. The Chickasaw also used special arrows fitted with a barbed point attached to a string to shoot the fish as they came to the surface.

Clothing

The basic wardrobe of the Chickasaw consisted of deerskin that was cut and then sewn using fish-bone needles and deer sinew. In the warmer months, the men wore deerskin breechcloths and bearskin moccasins. When hunting or traveling through the woods, they also wore deerskin leggings to protect themselves from brush and thorns. The women wore deerskin skirts and moccasins.

In the winter, deerskin shirts were added, along with long fur capes. The skins of panthers, beavers, deer, buffalo, and other animals were also used. The fur side was worn inside for warmth.

In addition to fashioning clothes from animal skins, the Chickasaw also wove material using fiber from mulberry bark. The feathers of turkeys, eagles, swans, and other birds were used to make decorative capes. A mantle of swan feathers was one of a warrior's prized possessions.

When going to war, or for certain special ceremonies, the Chickasaw men

painted their faces. The face paint reflected the clan of the wearer. They also wore nose and ear jewelry and tied eagle feathers in their hair.

Opposite: Chickasaw hunters spear fish that have been drugged and are floating on the water. Below: A Chickasaw woman and man in traditional dress.

Chickasaw women usually wore their hair straight. The Chickasaw men, however, shaved or plucked all the hair from the sides of their heads and wore it long on top. The long hair was often greased with bear oil to make it stand up.

Games

The Chickasaw game of *toli* was similar to the game of lacrosse that was played by many Native American tribes. However, *toli* was different in that players used two sticks, one in each hand. A *toli* stick had a round wooden shaft with a long, narrow wooden hoop at the end. The bottom of the hoop was crossed with deer sinew so the ball could not go through. The ball was made of deer hide stuffed with deer hair. The *toli* court was 500 feet long and had a goal at either end. When the Chickasaw played *toli*, one team painted themselves white.

Chunkey was another Chickasaw game. In this game, a stone ball was rolled down the playing field, and the men threw lances at the spot where they thought the ball would stop. The winner was the owner of the lance closest to the ball when it stopped.

Chickasaw men throw spears ahead of a rolling chunkey *ball.*

Above: Toli *sticks and a toli* ball. *Opposite: A Chickasaw boat builder hollows out a tree to make a dugout canoe.*

The *chunkey* stone was important and belonged to the whole village. It was kept for generations.

The Chickasaw also played *akabatle*. Unlike *toli* and *chunkey*, women also joined in the fun. In this game, all of the players gathered around a pole. On top of the pole was the likeness of a person. The object of the game was to hit the dummy with the ball. Games were played during celebrations, accompanied by big feasts.

Travel

The Chickasaw territory was marked by an extensive network of land trails, but the Chickasaw also traveled on the rivers of the area. They maintained a boat landing on the Mississippi River, which was the western boundary of their territory.

The Chickasaw used a number of different-sized boats, all of which were made the same way, as dugout canoes. To make a dugout canoe, the Chickasaw would first cut down a tree that was equal to the size boat they wanted to make. Next, they would build a fire right on the log. When the fire died down, they would scrape away the charred parts of the log. This process would continue until the log was hollowed out. Most of the Chickasaw boat builders used stone scrapers and clamshells to hollow out their boats. The largest Chickasaw dugouts held ten to fifteen people.

Warfare

War was simply a way of life for the Chickasaw. Boys began training at an early age to become warriors. Most Chickasaw warfare consisted of small raids to keep other tribes from using their territory. Although the Chickasaw had a relatively small tribe in numbers, they controlled a vast territory because of the strength of their warriors. Larger tribes attempted to defeat the Chickasaw without success. When the Chickasaw lands became part of the French holdings, the governor of Louisiana also tried to conquer the Chickasaw. After a number of failed attempts, he had to give up the idea.

Chickasaw warriors often formed into war parties of approximately fifty men and attacked neighboring tribes who had come onto their lands. Warriors were always anxious to perform acts of personal bravery. During raids, enemy men were killed, while women and children who were captured by the Chickasaw were kept as slaves. It was not unusual for Chickasaw warriors to torture their captives.

Warfare was a sacred responsibility of the Chickasaw. They observed a number of religious practices in their war preparations. Each warrior carried a sacred medicine bundle into battle along with his weapons. Their weapons of war were the bow and arrow, tomahawk, lance, and war club.

Political and Social Organization

The Chickasaw tribe was organized along two levels. The individual villages were independent, political units. However, the whole tribe was divided by clan and moiety. A moiety is a division of the tribe. Among the Chickasaw there were two moieties— the *Intcukwalipa* and the *Imosaktca*. At ceremonies the members of the *Imosaktca* would paint a small cross on their face above their cheekbone, while the *Intcukwalipa* would paint a cross below their cheekbone.

The *Imosaktca* was the dominant group. The main leader of the Chickasaw, the high *minko*, was always a member of the *Imosaktca*. Within the two moieties there were a number of clans. The number of clans varied to as many as fifteen. The clans were named after various animals, such as the raccoon, panther, and others. The members of each clan believed that they could trace their ancestry back to a common animal ancestor who founded the clan.

Opposite: A Chickasaw warrior of the **Intcukwalipa** *moiety paints a cross below his cheekbone. Below: A portrait of a young Chickasaw boy.*

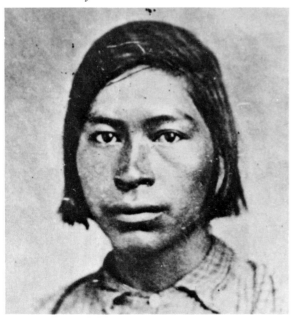

Children became members of their mother's clan and married someone from a different clan. Within a village each clan had a leader, called the *minko*. All the *minkos* that lived in one village ruled it together. They were responsible for settling disputes among members of the village. When crimes were committed among the Chickasaw, retaliation and revenge were expected. It was often the duty of the *minkos* to make sure the injured party sought adequate revenge for crimes committed against them. In case of murder, the family of the victim was expected to seek out and kill the murderer. If the murderer could not be found, his brother or another relative might be killed as a substitute.

Religious Life

For the Chickasaw, religion was an important part of every aspect of their lives. They believed that they lived in close proximity to the spirit world. Every action of a Chickasaw could affect the balance of their world. The most important spirit they believed in was called *Ababinili*. This was the spirit of the sky and the sun.

Every village of the Chickasaw had an altar dedicated to *Ababinili,* and it was the job of the village priests to tend the altar fires. Once a year the altar fires were put out and then relit. This was during the Chickasaw Green Corn Festival, which took place each year when the corn first began to

An elder is the first to be served fresh corn during the Green Corn Festival.

ripen. The festival was overseen by the *hopaye*, the high priests of the Chickasaw. One was chosen from each of the two moieties of the tribe.

During the Green Corn Festival the Chickasaw would fast for two days, then drink a potion the priests had prepared that would make them vomit. They did this to cleanse their systems of all impurities. After fasting and purging, a two-day feast would then be held. During the feast, fresh corn was always served.

The festival was a time when the tribal leaders came together. They would take care of any business that affected the whole tribe at this time. The festival was also a time of games and celebration.

In addition to *Ababinili*, the Chickasaw believed in other spirits. They believed that ten-foot-tall spirits, called *Lofas*, lived in the forests surrounding their villages. *Lofas* were thought to carry off women and cause hunters to be unsuccessful. They were also capable of causing other problems for people.

There were also good spirits, called *Iyaganashas*, believed to be three feet tall. The *Iyaganashas* helped the Chickasaw by sharing their knowledge with the people. They helped hunters learn the ways of their quarry, or prey. The *Iyaganashas* also gave Chickasaw healers the special knowledge they needed.

Chickasaw healers, called *aliktce*, were a combination of herbal doctors

21

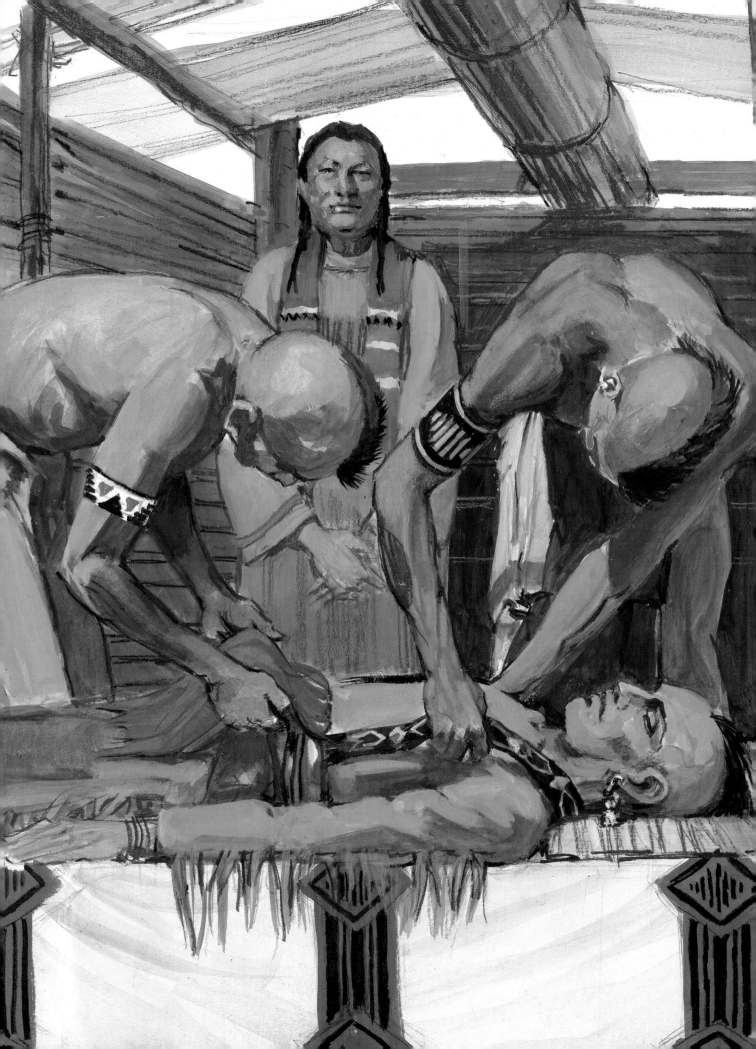

and priests. Nothing good or bad happened to a Chickasaw without the spirit world being involved. The *aliktce*, therefore, needed to attend to the spiritual side of their patients, as well as their physical ailments. The Chickasaw also believed in witches. The *aliktces* spent much of their time trying to undo evil that they believed witches had done. The *aliktces* were also adept at treating the wounds of the Chickasaw warriors. This was a job that kept them very busy.

The Chickasaw believed in an afterlife. The spirits of the Chickasaw went somewhere to the west, where they believed the souls of their ancestors dwelled. If the Chickasaw were bad during their lives, or if the proper ceremonies were not performed for their burials, their souls would not join their ancestors, but would be sent to a dark and evil place.

To prepare a dead person for his or her journey, a grave was dug inside the house of the person who had died. The body was washed and dressed. A warrior's weapons were buried with him, while a woman's prized possessions would join her. A supply of corn for the journey was also placed in the grave. The corpse was arranged in the grave in a sitting position facing west.

The family of the person who died would mourn for a year. The widow or widower was expected to cry over the grave at sunrise and sunset during the mourning period. Relatives took turns sleeping over the grave to keep evil spirits from interfering with the journey of the dead person's soul.

Opposite: The body of a Chickasaw warrior is prepared for burial.

European Contact

In 1539, the Spanish explorer Hernando De Soto landed in Florida searching for riches. By December of 1540, he had moved north to the lands of the Chickasaw. His force first made contact with the Chickasaw as they attempted to cross the Tombigbee River, and the Chickasaw attacked. The battle at the river lasted three days, until the Spanish finally crossed and captured a number of Chickasaw warriors.

In exchange for the captives, De Soto had the Chickasaw provide food and shelter for his men and their livestock. The Spanish force spent the winter of 1541 among the Chickasaw. In March, the Chickasaw decided to get rid of their unwanted guests and attacked the Spanish. The Chickasaw attack caught the Spanish by surprise. Twelve Spanish soldiers and many of their horses were killed. The Spanish were driven from their quarters in the middle of the night. Many fled from the attack without their clothes.

De Soto and his men spent a month at a nearby village and then returned south. This first contact between Europans and the Chickasaw had little impact. It did, however, alert the Chickasaw to the coming of the Europeans. They heard rumors from other Native Americans about the arrival of the English, the French, and more Spanish settlers, though they did not see any other Europeans for over 130 years.

In 1673, French explorers, Joliet and Marquette, passed through the lands of the Chickasaw on their trip down the Mississippi River. Then, in 1682, Robert Cavalier de la Salle and a force

of fifty-five French and Native Americans also came in contact with the Chickasaw. La Salle and his men had stopped at the Chickasaw Bluffs, overlooking the Mississippi River, the western boundary of the Chickasaw lands. One of La Salle's men, Pierre Prudhomme, got lost while hunting. A stockade was quickly built on the bluffs and called Fort Prudhomme. La Salle and his men stored their supplies in the fort while they searched for Prudhomme. During the search they came in contact with the Chickasaw. La Salle sent presents as offerings of peace. Prudhomme was found, and La Salle's expedition continued without incident.

In 1698, two English traders, Thomas Welch and Anthony Dodsworth, began trading with the Chickasaw. The Chickasaw were eager for European goods. The women wanted cloth and metal farm tools; the men, guns and other metal weapons. The Chickasaw also wanted brass wire to make jewelry. They traded deerskin and slaves for the manufactured goods that Welch and Dodsworth brought. The Native American slaves that the Chickasaw traded had been captured in raids on their enemies. The English traders went to the Carolinas and sold some of the slaves locally. The rest were shipped to the slave markets in the West Indies.

In North America during the seventeenth and eighteenth centuries, there were problems among the European countries trying to establish colonies.

Chickasaw warriors and Spanish soldiers battle at the Tombigbee River in 1540.

Major conflicts arose between the British and the French in particular, both of whom tried to make allies among the Native Americans. One of their methods was to encourage the Native Americans to attack each other. Although the Chickasaw were not very close to the areas of settlement, they still got caught up in the conflicts.

The Chickasaw were loyal to the English traders who visited their lands. They preferred the English goods and prices to those of the French. The French had established a number of settlements along the Gulf Coast. In 1702, the French invited the Chickasaw to send representatives to a meeting in Mobile, Alabama. They tried to convince the Chickasaw to stop fighting with their neighbors—the

Choctaw—and ally themselves with the French. The Chickasaw chose to remain loyal to the English.

The French encouraged tribes loyal to them to attack the Chickasaw. Then they tried to conquer the Chickasaw in the Battle of Akia in 1736, but they were defeated. During this period, the Chickasaw became very dependent on European goods and began to lose some of their traditional ways.

The British finally prevailed and won what is now called the French and Indian War. In the Peace of Paris in 1763, the French gave up all claims in North America east of the Mississippi. They also ceded the land to the west to

25

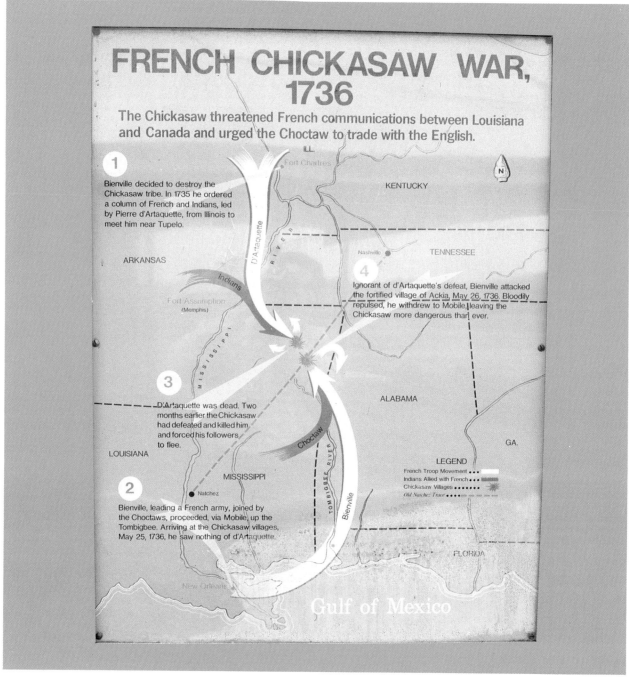

A chart depicts the battle between the French and the Chickasaw in 1736. The French were unsuccessful in their attempt to surprise the Chickasaw and were defeated.

Spain. The peace settlement, however, did not end the problems that Native Americans faced. More settlers arrived and they all wanted land. They often took what they wanted, with no consideration for the Native Americans who had been living there.

Despite the end of the French and Indian War, the Chickasaw continued to raid neighboring tribes. The demands for European goods among the Chickasaw increased, and the only commodity that they had to trade was slaves. The Chickasaw began raiding villages just to take captives for the slave trade.

The Chickasaw also acquired horses and African slaves from the English traders. Soon they were raiding tribes across the Mississippi to steal horses. They became excellent horsemen and even developed their own breed of horses, called Chickasaws. These horses were well known throughout the Mississippi River area.

The Chickasaw and the United States

The Chickasaw faced a new challenge from the newly created United States. During the American Revolution, the Chickasaw sided with the British. Toward the end of the Revolution, in 1780, the colonials launched a campaign to subdue the Chickasaw. This first attempt to invade the Chickasaw lands was unsuccessful.

In 1783, the Revolution ended. The Treaty of Paris recognized the existence of the United States and defined its boundaries. The Chickasaw lands were inside the boundaries of the United States. Both the Spanish and the Americans urged the Chickasaw to sign treaties. Some Chickasaw favored the United States, while others favored the Spanish. The Chickasaw finally signed a treaty with the state of Virginia. The state claimed a vast territory to the west of its present borders.

Only one year later, in 1784, the Chickasaw also signed a treaty with Spain. Then between 1801 and 1818, the Chickasaw signed four more treaties with the United States. In each treaty, the Chickasaw made concessions.

In 1801, the Chickasaw accepted $700 in exchange for the rights to build a wagon road through their territory. In 1806, they gave up claim to all lands north of the Tennessee River.

For this they received $20,000. In 1816, the Chickasaw gave up claims to all land south of the Tennessee River, to the west bank of the Tombigbee River. For this they received a promise of $12,000 a year for ten years. In 1819, they again gave up even more of their land.

For the land-hungry settlers on the western frontier of the United States, this was still not enough. Native Americans throughout the Southeast were being forced off their lands. In 1830, the Congress of the United States passed the Indian Removal Act. This made it legal for the government to force the Native Americans of the Southeast to give up their lands. The law also set up the Indian Territory in what is today Oklahoma. Tribes that were forced to leave the Southeast were to be given lands in Oklahoma.

Most Native Americans in the Southeast did not agree with this law. However, President Andrew Jackson was not interested in what the Native Americans thought. He even defied the Supreme Court, who ruled in favor of the Cherokee when they tried to prevent their own removal. The removal of the Five Civilized Tribes from the Southeast has become known as the Trail of Tears.

For the Chickasaw and other tribes that were forced to move to the Indian Territory, this was a time of extreme hardship. The first Chickasaw to head west were a group of 450 people. They were escorted by General John Millard, who said he would hurry the Chickasaw at the point of a bayonet if he needed to. The group crossed the Mississippi on July 4, 1837. They did not reach Fort Towson in the Choctaw territory

The official seal of the Chickasaw nation.

1838 killed approximately 500 Chickasaw. Much of the food they received was spoiled and unfit to eat. Some of the food they paid for was never sent to them. Traders who were greedy made fortunes by supplying poor-quality food. Sometimes these traders just took the money and did not deliver anything. For their first years in the Indian Territory, the Chickasaw lived in five camps run by the federal government.

Over time, they moved out of the camps and onto their own lands in south-central Oklahoma, just east of what is today Ardmore, Oklahoma. By the mid-1850s, almost all of the Chickasaw lived in their own section of the Indian Territory. Most of the Chickasaw became farmers, though some established other businesses such as stores, lumber mills, and cotton gins. Some Chickasaw bought slaves and had large farms.

Most Chickasaw, especially those of mixed blood, had given up their traditional lifestyle by this time. Many built log cabins to live in and dressed like the non-Native Americans who shared the frontier with them. Most Chickasaw had no formal education.

At the time of their removal, the Chickasaw had been included with the Choctaw. They were not formally recognized as a tribe. Yet in 1855, the Chickasaw signed a treaty with the government that again made them an independent tribe from the Choctaw. A year later, they established their own constitution and set up a tribal government to oversee their affairs.

During the Civil War, Confederate troops from Texas invaded much of the Indian Territory. Most of the Native

until September 5th. Along the way many Chickasaw died, some of dysentery, and others of malnutrition.

In the fall of 1837, approximately 4,000 Chickasaw were put in detention camps and then sent to the Indian Territory. Three thousand of these Chickasaw were fortunate, and were transported to Fort Coffee by boat. The trip upriver took about ten days. The other 1,000 Chickasaw traveled overland. It took them about a month to get to Fort Coffee. Fortunately, the Chickasaw did not lose as many of their people on this trip west as some of the other tribes did.

After the Native Americans arrived in Oklahoma, they discovered that their troubles had just begun. Disease, poor living conditions, and malnutrition plagued them. A smallpox epidemic in

Americans allied themselves with the Confederates. In February 1864, however, Union soldiers invaded the Chickasaw lands. By July, the Chickasaw had surrendered to the Union and were forced to cede all lands that they had leased from the government.

The next major problem for the Chickasaw, and all Native Americans living on their own lands, was the General Allotment Act of 1897. The Dawes Act, as it was also called, deeded tribal lands to individual Native Americans. Any surplus land could be sold. The point of the Dawes Act was to eliminate Indian tribes and make all Native Americans part of the mainstream culture.

The Chickasaw resisted the allotment of their lands until 1906. At that time 1,538 full-blooded Chickasaw, 4,146 mixed-blood Chickasaw, and 635 whites married to Chickasaw were entitled to an allotment. Each person was to receive 320 acres. In March 1906, the Chickasaw government was dissolved once again. On November 16, 1907, the Indian Territory and Oklahoma Territory combined to become the state of Oklahoma.

Many of the allotments were later sold. Other Chickasaw were cheated out of their lands. The government bought back 3 million acres from the Chickasaw for $19 million, and every Chickasaw received $1,075 from the settlement. Some Chickasaw were lucky, and oil was discovered under their land. Most Chickasaw, however, remained poor. In 1958, a bill was introduced in the U.S. Congress that would have eliminated the Five Civilized Tribes. This bill was not passed.

The Chickasaw Today

After the attempt in 1958 to eliminate the Five Civilized Tribes, the federal government changed its attitude toward Native Americans. The government realized that Native American culture was of value. A period of Native American self-determination followed.

The government stopped trying to make Native Americans just like everyone else, and began to try to help them raise their standard of living and level of education, while maintaining their unique cultural heritage. For the Chickasaw this meant the re-establishment of their tribal identity.

In 1971, Overton James was elected governor of the Chickasaw tribe, the first Chickasaw governor since their government had been dissolved in 1906. James did many things to help the Chickasaw. He got the government to set up a Chickasaw housing authority, and also started a newsletter that later became *The Chickasaw Times.*

In 1975, Congress passed the Indian Self-Determination Act, which provided guidelines and funds for Native Americans to take care of themselves. Governor James was able to use the funds provided by the act to make improvements for the Chickasaw.

Today, the Chickasaw are pushing for the education of the younger members of their tribe. They also have programs to help older members become better educated. There are two Chickasaw adult education centers, as well as a tutoring program to help Chickasaw who have dropped out of school to study for a high-school equivalency exam.

The Chickasaw capitol building in Tishomingo, Oklahoma, the capital of the Chickasaw nation. The Chickasaw purchased the building in 1989 from the state of Oklahoma.

In 1987, the Chickasaw adopted a new constitution that gave them even more control over their own lives. The Chickasaw have also created the Museum of Chickasaw Indian Culture, which strives to preserve as much of the unique culture of the Chickasaw as possible.

According to the 1990 U.S. Census, there are 20,631 people who are Chickasaw, 12,772 of whom live in Oklahoma. More than 2,000 Chickasaw live in both Texas and California, and the rest live throughout the United States. Like many Native American tribes, the Chickasaw were almost eliminated by government policies. However, the Chickasaw still face many problems, but are meeting their challenges with the fierceness and determination they once showed as the most feared warriors of the Southeast.

Chronology

1540 Spanish explorer Hernando De Soto makes the first European contact with the Chickasaw.

1673 French explorers Marquette and Joliet pass through the Chickasaw territory.

1682 French explorer La Salle makes contact with the Chickasaw.

1698 Thomas Welch and Anthony Dodsworth bring English goods to the Chickasaw and exchange them for deer hides and slaves.

1702 The French invite Chickasaw leaders to Mobile, Alabama, for a meeting.

1736 The Chickasaw defeat the French in the Battle of Akia.

1780 American colonists unsuccessfully invade the Chickasaw territory. The Chickasaw remain loyal to Britain during the Revolution.

1783 The Chickasaw sign a peace treaty with the new state of Virginia.

1784 The Chickasaw sign a peace treaty with Spain.

1801 The Chickasaw sign a treaty with the United States giving up claim to all land north of the Tennessee River.

1816 The Chickasaw sign a treaty with the United States giving up claim to all land from the west bank of the Tombigbee River to the Tennessee River.

1819 The Chickasaw sign a treaty with the United States giving up claim to more of their traditional lands.

1830 The U.S. Congress passes the Indian Removal Act.

1837 The first group of Chickasaw are removed to Choctaw lands in the Indian Territory.

1838 Five hundred Chickasaw die of smallpox during relocation.

1855 The Chickasaw sign a treaty with the United States that separates them from the Choctaw in the Indian Territory.

1856 The Chickasaw establish their own constitution and a tribal government.

1864 The Chickasaw surrender to Union soldiers during the Civil War.

1906 The Chickasaw government is dissolved and their lands allotted to individual members of the tribe.

1971 Overton James is elected first Chickasaw tribal governor since 1906.

1987 The Chickasaw adopt a new constitution.

INDEX

Acknowledgments and Photo Credits
Cover and all artwork by Richard Smolinski
Pages 16, 26, 38, 30: Courtesy Chickasaw Nation; p.18: Photograph courtesy of Museum of
the American Indian, Heye Foundation.
Map by Blackbirch Graphics, Inc.